Beginner's Guide to
Silk Shading

Clare Hanham

SEARCH PRESS

First published in Great Britain 2007

Search Press Limited
Wellwood, North Farm Road,
Tunbridge Wells, Kent TN2 3DR

ISBN-10: 1-84448-112-3
ISBN-13: 978-1-84448-112-5

The Publishers and author can accept no responsibility for any
consequences arising from the information, advice or instructions
given in this publication.

Readers are permitted to reproduce any of the items/patterns in
this book for their personal use, or for the purposes of selling for
charity, free of charge and without the prior permission of the
Publishers. Any use of the items/patterns for commercial purposes
is not permitted without the prior permission of the Publishers.

Suppliers
If you have difficulty in obtaining any of the materials and
equipment mentioned in this book, then please visit the Search
Press website for details of suppliers:
www.searchpress.com

Acknowledgements

*I would like to thank my parents, my brother,
Tim, and friends who have encouraged and
inspired me to follow my dreams to become a
professional embroiderer.*

*I would also like to thank my form tutor,
Bet Baker, who started me off with cross
stitch at the age of eleven; Lee Purnell for
his help and friendship, the Royal School
of Needlework for my training and all the
ladies who have attended my classes for their
enthusiasm and support.*

*Last but not least I would like to thank
Search Press for giving me the opportunity to
write this book.*

Publisher's note
All the step-by-step photographs in this book feature the
author, Clare Hanham, demonstrating silk shading. No
models have been used.

Contents

Introduction

Silk was discovered in China over 46 centuries ago, making it one of the oldest fibres known to man. There are references to silk in the Old Testament of the Bible. Its strength and sheen made it ideal for embroidery.

Embroidery worked in silk goes back many centuries. The silk shading technique uses long and short stitch worked in silk or cotton thread. There are historical embroideries that appear to be shaded, but these are not always worked in long and short stitch – sometimes different coloured rows of split stitch worked tightly together create a shaded effect.

Early embroidery was mainly ecclesiastical and worked professionally. The Egyptian Copts of the 4th century, who were Christians, created embroideries showing saints, whose robes and faces were shaded in long and short stitch, often within a circular design. These were mainly worked in silk but there are a few surviving that were worked in wool.

Silk shading then dips in and out of history. In the 13th century very fine embroidery with an emphasis on goldwork developed, but this was brought to a halt in the early 14th century by the Black Death, which led to a shortage in workers. Ecclesiastical embroidery was still in high demand, so people returned to quicker embroidery techniques, such as long and short stitch.

Embroidery became more domestic around the Tudor period and by the Stuart period long and short stitch was being used on a variety of styles of work. This work was often done by young girls as a sample of their skills, or by ladies of 'high birth' as a pastime.

The three-dimensional form of embroidery, stumpwork, became popular. This was worked in silk and used a variety of different stitches including long and short stitch. The designs were normally biblical or showed royalty. The work was often made into beautiful caskets or mirror frames, many of which can be seen in museums.

Later in the 17th century, crewel embroidery became popular, and long and short stitch was worked in the fine crewel wool that the technique was named after. Large leaves and pods inspired by the Indian 'tree of life' designs that had travelled across to Europe with silk imports were embroidered, sometimes completely in long and short stitch. Large curtains and bed hangings in this style were made for great houses around England.

The 18th century saw a drop in the popularity of long and short stitch as canvas work became the vogue. In the nineteenth century, very fine silk shading was worked on to beautifully painted silk backgrounds. The designs were normally pastoral or biblical with figures whose clothes and drapery were shaded to show every fold. The hands and faces were finely painted, but the ground areas and any other main features were often worked in long and short stitch.

Long and short stitch is still done today as a part of other techniques and in a variety of different types of thread, as it has been throughout history. The term 'silk shading' is slightly misleading, as it is more often than not worked these days in cotton thread, as in this book.

This antique piece of embroidery, mainly worked in long and short stitch, was among a bundle of fabrics and threads given to me by Mrs Elizabeth Boswell. The flower head and the bud are particularly beautiful and show off the use of silk shading.

I was introduced to silk shading when I studied as an apprentice at the Royal School of Needlework in London. It is a technique we learn very early on as apprentices and is used frequently throughout our training. For our first two projects, we worked the stitch in wool and for the third, we worked a flower of our choice in stranded cottons, with many needles, all with different shades of thread being attached to the work at one time. I worked fuchsias in my favourite colours of deep pinks and purples.

I find shading very relaxing and satisfying to work, as once you get the hang of it, it can grow quite quickly and, with the right shades, look stunning. I really enjoy watching the design grow as you add in colours and blend the threads.

I began to teach silk shading soon after I started my freelance career as people were fascinated and inspired by the technique, and it really is achievable for any stitcher.

The subjects for shading, as with most embroidery, are endless. I keep scrapbooks with pictures from magazines, postcards and greeting cards – in fact anything that inspires me. These scrapbooks are a fantastic source of inspiration and very useful when you want to find a design out of season, for instance a snowdrop in June or a tulip in December.

This book aims to take you through the basics of long and short stitch and on into a variety of projects, which can be used in many ways. Shading works well on many items, not just pictures for your walls, but for cards, pincushions, bags, purses, box lids and bookmarks.

I hope this book gives you confidence in your stitching, inspires you for hours and enables you to enjoy silk shading as much as I do.

Happy stitching!

Clare x

Opposite
A selection of items stitched using silk shading.

Materials

Fabric

Silk shading can be done on a variety of fabrics. I would normally choose a plain fabric so that it does not distract from the stitching. However, the slightly mottled cottons can give a modern look.

Fabrics can also be layered, so for sheen, use organza over a coloured background. Denim is also a great sturdy background fabric to work with.

I generally like to use silk dupion, as I like the way the slubs add texture to the fabric, without distracting the eye from the stitching too much.

Unless you choose a very heavy fabric, it is always best to back it with a piece of calico or heavy cotton. However, if your calico is very rough, it may show through a pale fabric and it may slightly change the colour. Backing fabric helps to take the weight of the stitches and stops the fabric from puckering around the edge of the stitching. The projects in this book are all worked on silk dupion backed with calico.

When choosing the colour of your background fabric, place the threads you are going to use on to it. This will give you a good idea of how it will look. Check which colours are going to be at the edge of your design and are therefore going to be seen against the fabric.

Pale shades are the most natural choice for background fabric, but sometimes strong, dark-coloured fabrics work well as they can really throw the stitching forward. With darker fabrics, the background fabric may show through between the stitches, so you have to be extra careful when you are stitching.

Try using complementary colours such as blue and orange, yellow and purple and red and green together.

8

Thread

Despite the name silk shading, you do not have to work in silk! Shading can be done in any thread. All the projects in this book are worked in normal stranded cotton embroidery threads, using one of the six strands. This may seem very fine, but it quickly builds up and gives a smoother overall look to the work.

Tip
When splitting your threads, hold them between your thumb and finger and pull one strand out upwards. The rest of the threads will ravel up underneath. If you try and pull a strand out sideways, it will twist itself up to the other strands and be harder to separate.

Needles and pins

The projects in this book are all stitched in one strand of stranded cotton, so I have used no. 9 embroidery needles. These are sharp with a long eye, which is easier for threading. The needles that are called 'sharps' are also sharp, but have a smaller, rounder eye. You can use these, but they are harder to thread. I find the finer the needle, the better, as it will not make such large holes in the fabric, but obviously use something that you can thread!

Beware of old needles that have developed rusty patches and lost their coating, as they will be harder to work with. Also, if you have a needle that seems to be catching at the tip, get rid of it.

For silk shading it is best to have several needles, so that you can have all your colours threaded up.

You will need dressmaker's pins to pin your backing fabric and fabric together before you start stitching.

Frames

It is essential to work silk shading in a tight frame, as if you do not, the length and the amount of stitches will pucker the fabric.

There are a variety of frames available. Wooden ring frames are great for getting the work really tight as you can tighten them using a screwdriver. They are available in a variety of sizes. Use one that leaves plenty of room around your design.

Seat frames are great to use, as by sitting on the base, both your hands are left free for stitching.

Bigger designs may need to be worked in a slate frame. These will also hold your work nice and tight, but they take longer to set up as you have to sew your fabric to the frame.

All the projects were worked in ring frames except for the Dog Roses project, which was worked in a slate frame because of its size.

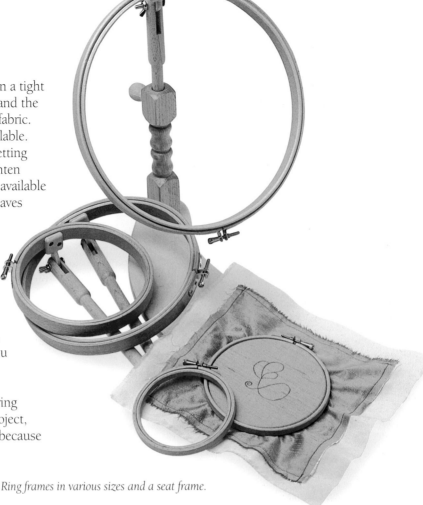

Ring frames in various sizes and a seat frame.

Beads

Seed beads, bugles and small sequins can be used to embellish and enhance your embroidery. Seed beads are used in the Climbing Leaves project on page 24, and on the card and pincushion on page 27. Small sequins and beads set off the silk shading on the denim bag shown on page 39.

A selection of seed beads, bugles and small sequins.

Other materials

Light box This is used to help you trace designs on to fabric. They are available from good camera shops and craft suppliers in a variety of sizes.

Tracing paper You will need this to draw your design on, so that you can then trace it on to your fabric.

Black fine line pen Trace your design on to the tracing paper with a black fine line pen. This gives crisp, dark lines and should not leave marks on your fabric.

Low tack tape or **masking tape** Tape your design to the light box or window with either of these, as sticky tape will leave marks.

Pencil and **coloured pencils** You will need pencils for designing, and also for tracing the design on to your fabric and drawing on directional lines etc. A softer pencil is easiest to use, but if you are using pale threads, the graphite may come off on them. In this case use a coloured drawing pencil. Light blue is good with paler fabrics, and white or yellow for darker fabrics.

Shower cap These are great for slipping over ring frames to keep the work clean while you are not stitching.

Screwdriver A screwdriver is essential for tightening your ring frame. Make sure you have the right size for your screw.

Scissors Small, sharp pointed scissors are needed for cutting embroidery threads. Scissors with a slight curve on the tip are good for cutting threads close to the fabric. You will need larger dressmaker's scissors for cutting your fabric. Use separate scissors for paper.

Tweezers If you have tacked on your design (see page 20), tweezers are useful for removing bits of tissue paper left over when you tear off the tracing.

Thimbles You may need a thimble to protect your pushing fingers, especially if you are using very fine needles.

Iron Press your fabrics before you draw the design on. Check that your iron and ironing board are clean before you do so.

White tissue paper To keep your work clean as you stitch it, place a piece of tissue paper in between the two rings of your ring frame when you push it together. Then rip a small hole over the area you are working. You can also use tissue paper to wrap your work in when you are not working on it.

A shower cap, used to cover your ring frame to protect your embroidery when you are not working on it.

A light box, fine line pen, tracing paper, white tissue paper, pencils, low tack tape, scissors, thimbles, tweezers, a screwdriver and an iron.

Techniques

If you are already a stitcher, you will have developed your own techniques, however, these are the methods used by professionals – they may help you to produce even more beautiful work. If you have never stitched before, they are a great way to start!

Casting on

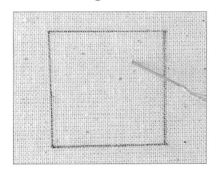

1. Start by knotting the end of your thread, leaving a little tail at the end.

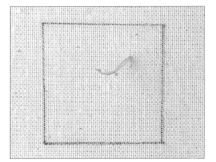

2. Take the needle down through the fabric, leaving the knot on the top. You can do this in any area of the design that is later going to be stitched over.

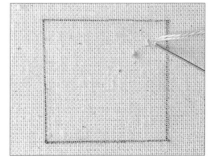

3. Work two small stitches near the knot.

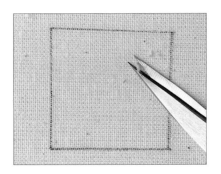

4. With small, sharp scissors, cut the knot off. You can hold it by its tail to snip beneath the knot. Pull on your thread to make sure it is firmly attached before you start stitching.

Split stitch

This is a very simple stitch, but makes an enormous difference to the quality of your finished piece. It can be used as a stitch on its own, but also as an outlining stitch underneath long and short stitch to help give a nice, crisp shape. Split stitch is worked around the outer edges of silk shading. You work the split stitch for each little area as you are going to stitch it.

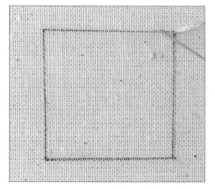

1. Having cast on, come up at the beginning of the line you wish to stitch. Make a small stitch, taking the needle forwards.

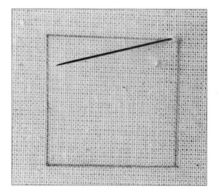

2. Take the needle back down beneath the fabric and bring it up halfway through your first stitch.

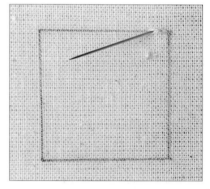

3. Make another stitch, again taking the needle forwards along the line and down through the fabric. Come up halfway through the stitch.

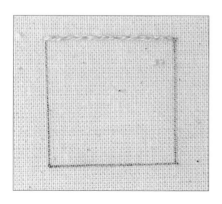

4. Work along the line in this way until it is complete.

Tip
You only need to split stitch around the outer edges as you work them. Any overlapping areas should be split stitched all the way round. See pages 22 and 23, steps 1 and 8.

Long and short stitch

Worked straight

Long and short stitch is great for filling big areas or delicately shading small areas. It can be worked with as many different shades as you like. If you have a range of colours, it works well to take every other colour, for example if you have shade numbers 1 to 6, you would use 2, 4 and 6 or 1, 3 and 5. However this is just a guide and sometimes colours from other ranges have to be brought in.

One of the most common mistakes with this technique is to work regimented long, short, long, short stitches. This creates a striped effect instead of shading. The stitches only need to be slightly varied in length, so that a solid line is not formed. Longer stitches give a smoother overall look, so do not be afraid to stitch them long.

To guide you with direction and colours, you can draw on to your fabric with pencil. The stitches should overlap by a third, so divide the area you are stitching into as many colours as you have and draw lines on. Then make sure that your stitches are worked over these lines. This will allow for the next colour to come into it by a third without losing the amount of the first colour that you wanted.

I always work my shading in a single strand of thread, as this gives it a fine, smooth look. Using two threads may make it quicker to work but gives a lumpier, heavier look as the threads twist together.

Tip
Long and short stitch is meant to look as natural as possible, so relax when you do it, and do not worry too much about whether you are doing each stitch in the right place. As with many techniques, it takes practice!

1. Draw a 2.5cm (1in) square on to the fabric and divide it into three equal sections. Select three shades to work with, a dark, medium and a light. With the lightest, work a split stitch edge across the top line of the square. To keep the correct angle for the area you are stitching, work your first stitch in the middle of the area as a guide. Come up into the fabric below the first line and go down over the split stitch edge.

Tip
Stitching from the middle to the left and then from the middle to the right helps to keep your stitching at the correct angle.

14

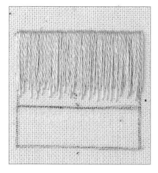

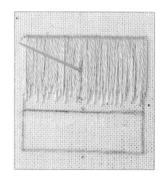

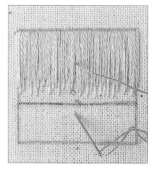

2. Work out towards one side. For each stitch, come up in the fabric and down over the split stitch edge. Each stitch should be a slightly different length to the one next to it, but none should fall short of the first pencil line. Work the stitches really close together so there are no gaps between them.

3. Go back to the centre and work in the same way, going out in the other direction. You may find this direction harder, one side is always easier! Remember to put lots of stitches in really close together.

4. Cast on a single strand of your medium shade thread in the area below the stitching that you have just done. Bring the needle up a third of the way into the light stitches, in the middle as before. It does not matter if you split the light stitches.

5. Take the stitch down below the next pencil line into the fabric. This is the opposite direction to the first row of stitches and all consecutive rows are worked in this way, up in the stitches and down into the fabric.

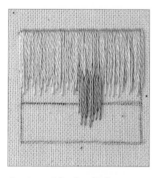

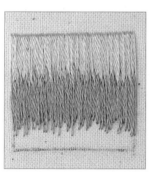

6. As with the light colour, stitch out to one side. This time you need to remember to stagger the length of the stitches at both ends.

7. Go back to the middle and repeat as before, working out in the other direction. If you find that stitching this colour creates gaps in between the pale stitches above, this may be because the stitches of the first row were not packed in tightly enough.

8. Using a single strand of your dark thread, work the bottom row. Come up into the middle row of stitches and go down over the pencil line at the bottom.

9. As you have no free space to cast off, turn your work over and weave the thread into the back.

Worked in a petal shape

As few shapes are perfectly square and straight, you need to learn how to vary the angle of your shading, so that you can stitch around different shapes. The main silk shading technique is the same, but you may need to add extra stitches, spread them out or tuck them in slightly.

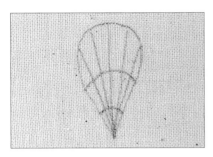

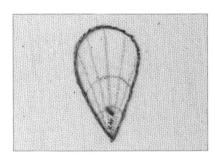

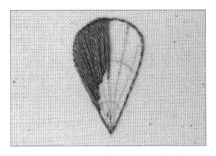

1. Draw a petal shape on your fabric and divide it into three sections, echoing the curve of the petal. Then draw direction lines to guide your stitches. Draw the central one in first so that it is vertical, then splay them out to either side from the bottom point. Select three shades of thread to work with, a dark, a medium and a light.

2. Using a single strand of the lightest colour, cast on in the shape with a knot and two small securing stitches. Split stitch all the way around the edge.

3. Bring the needle up just below the top pencil line in the middle and take it down over the split stitch edge. Work out to one side, varying the length of the stitches. Pack the stitches in tightly inside the petal, but spread them slightly as they go over the split stitch edge. Follow the directional pencil lines. All stitches should be angled towards the point at the bottom.

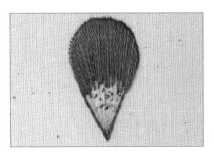

4. Work out to the second side in the same way. Remember to keep the stitches nice and long and vary the length at the bottom.

5. Work the medium shade out to either side from the middle, staggering the length at both ends. The stitches need to be splayed out when you bring them up into the light colour and tucked closer together as you take them down into the fabric over the second pencil line.

6. Using the dark thread, fill in the last little area. You will need fewer stitches, so place them carefully. As they are all going down towards one point, stop some of them slightly short so that it does not get too bulky at the point. Cast off by weaving into the back.

Stem stitch

Stem stitch can be used for stems and tendrils. It can be worked in a single strand of thread or in multiple strands for a thicker line.

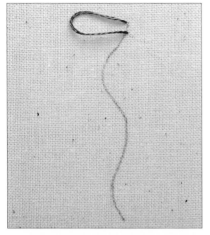

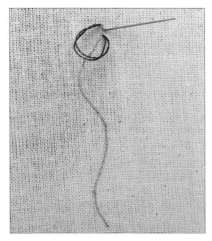

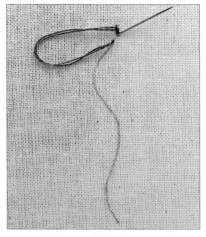

1. Cast on along the line you are going to stitch, or in any other area nearby that you are going to stitch over. Bring the needle up in the fabric and make a stitch, leaving a loop.

2. Bring the needle up halfway through the loop and pull the thread of the loop through.

3. Take the needle forward making a second stitch, again leaving a loop of thread. Bring the needle back up halfway through the stitch, pulling the loop through.

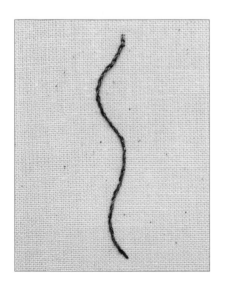

4. Continue stitching in this way, making sure that you always bring your needle up to the same side of the loop, so that you create a line of slanting stitches that are all slanting in the same direction.

This flower features long and short stitch worked in petal shapes and a stem stitch stalk.

Chain stitch

Chain stitch gives a thicker line than stem stitch and is also good for stems and tendrils.

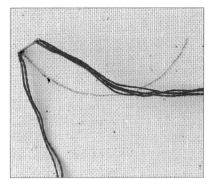 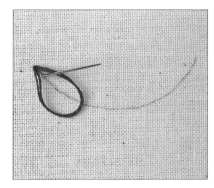 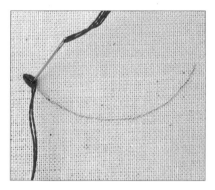

1. Cast on along the line you are going to stitch, or in any nearby area that will be stitched. Bring the needle up and holding a loop out with your thumb, take the needle back down into the same hole.

2. Bring the needle back up into the loop and then pull the thread through, tightening the loop.

3. Take the needle down back into the same loop. The thread then creates a new loop for you to hold with your thumb. Bring the needle up ahead of itself on the line to hold this loop in place as you pull it through. Continue along the line.

The finished shape worked in chain stitch.

18

French knots

These can be used for pips, seeds and decoration. They look great when worked in groups and can be mixed with beads. The more strands of thread you use, the bigger the knots will be.

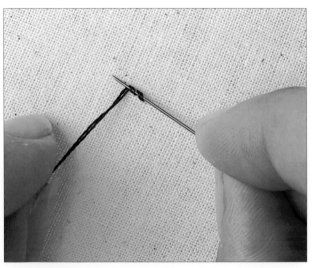

1. Bring the needle up. Holding the thread taught, wrap it twice around the tip of the needle.

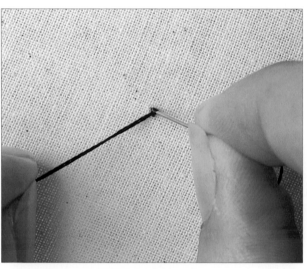

2. Put the tip of the needle into the fabric and pull the thread tight, so that your little knot is formed before you pull the thread though.

3. Repeat to make multiple knots.

How to start

This mini project takes you through the best ways to prepare your fabrics and work the design.

With silk shading it is important to work areas that are furthest back first. Look at the design and decide which areas are behind, and which are in front. The areas are then stitched in order, starting from the back. The split stitch edges are worked as you do each area, allowing each one to sit slightly proud of the area behind it. This helps to give a three-dimensional effect.

The stylised flower design has overlapping petals so that you can have a go at working a design in order. It is perfect for a small picture or a special card.

The pattern for the mini-project, shown full size. The numbers tell you the order of stitching.

Transferring a design

Using a light box or window

Trace the design with a black pen. Tape the tracing to the light box or a window with masking tape. Place your fabric over the design and using a pencil, trace the design on to your fabric. This should work with most pale coloured fabrics. If your design is going to be worked in very pale colours, use a blue pencil, as graphite can make the threads dirty.

> ### Tip
> If it is a dull day and you do not have a light box, try using a television!

Tacking the design instead of drawing

If your fabric is too dark or too heavy a weave to see through, the design can be tacked on instead.

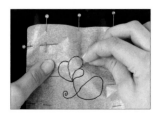

1. Trace the design on to tissue paper and pin it to your fabric. Tack around the design in fairly small stitches in a contrasting thread.

2. When the tacking of the design is complete, tear the tracing paper off. Use tweezers to pull off any small bits that are difficult to remove.

Preparing the fabric

Careful preparation of your fabric can make all the difference to the finished work. If you are embroidering on to a fine fabric, you will need to back it with another stronger fabric such as calico or heavy cotton, to help take the weight of the stitches. This will prevent the fabric from puckering around the stitching.

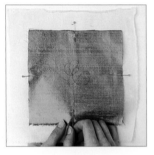

1. Pin your fabric on to a piece of backing fabric. Start with a pin on each side. Make sure that the two pieces are lying together on the grain.

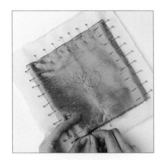

2. Pin outwards to the corners. This pushes any creases out. Pin with the pins horizontal to the fabric.

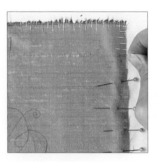

3. Stitch the two pieces of fabric together. This can be done in a variety of ways. One way is a long and short stitch, coming up in to the main fabric and going down into the background fabric.

4. The other way is herringbone stitch. Again it is always best to start in the middle of an edge and stitch outwards. You can also use a sewing machine on zigzag stitch.

Framing up

It is essential to work silk shading in a ring frame to prevent the fabric from puckering as you stitch. You need to keep the fabric in the ring drum tight, so keep tightening it up as you work as it will loosen over time. Use a screwdriver to tighten the screw. You can wrap your ring frame in strips of calico or bias binding to help it to grip the fabric, especially if you are working on a satin or silky fabric.

1. Place one half of the ring underneath the fabric and the other on top. Push the two rings together. It is best to push your fabric into the ring as tightly as you can to start with, then tighten it further.

2. Use a screwdriver to tighten the screw. The dumpy-handled type are good as they fit easily into your sewing kit. Be careful not to use one with the wrong size tip, as this will ruin the screw in your frame.

Silk shading the design

This motif is stitched using four colours: light pink, medium pink, dark pink and brown.

Tip
Always bring threads that you are not currently using up to the front of your work, in an area that will be stitched over later, so that you do not leave little holes around the edges of your work.

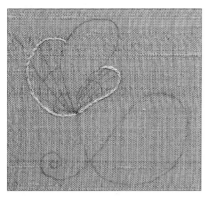

1. Using the lightest thread, cast on one strand and split stitch around the outer edge of the two outer petals. You do not need to stitch around the inner edge, as that will be stitched when you work the front petal. Draw on the direction lines and divide the area into three sections horizontally.

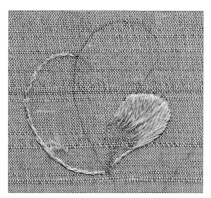

2. Begin the silk shading using a single strand of light pink in the smallest petal. Work your stitches out over the split stitch edge.

3. Shade in the medium pink, coming up in the light pink stitches and going down into the fabric. Remember to echo the outside shape of the petal with the dark stitches and to vary their length at the bottom.

4. Work the dark pink down to the bottom of the petal.

5. Add a tiny bit of brown shading at the base of the smallest petal. Then work the first stage of the far left-hand petal in light pink.

6. Continue the shading with the medium pink. Remember to vary the height of the stitches when you come up into the light pink to give a feathered look.

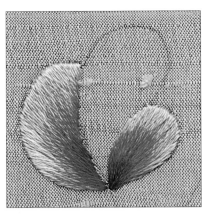

7. Add the dark pink shading to the left-hand petal, stitching to the bottom of the petal.

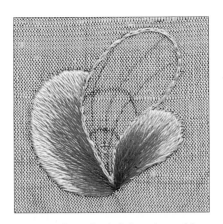

8. Complete the left-hand petal by shading with a little bit of brown at the base. Draw direction lines for the middle petal. Split stitch all round the edge in light pink.

9. Work the first layer of shading in the middle petal. You can keep the stitches at the sides fairly vertical – they will still cover the split stitch edge.

10. Shade in the medium pink. Fan the stitches out at the top and tuck them together at the bottom to get the angle.

11. Add the dark pink in the middle petal and complete the flower by adding a touch of brown at the base of the petal.

12. For the finishing touch on the flower, add a small copper sequin and bead. Using the brown thread, come up through the sequin and bead and then take the needle back down through the sequin only. Cast your brown thread off into the back of the design.

Tip
If your thread becomes tired looking when you are stitching, cast it off and use a new one. Also, if you have done a lot of unpicking, also use a new thread.

13. Complete the embroidery by working the stem stitch in two strands of brown.

Climbing Leaves

This project has three quirky leaf shapes that are perfect for practising your shading. The angle of the stitches is very gentle and stays the same all the way down each side of each leaf. This allows you to concentrate on the blending of the colours. This sample is worked on a calico-backed silk in various lime greens, but why not use three of your favourite colours?

You will need
Off-white silk dupion,
10 x 20cm (4 x 7⁷/₈in)
Calico, bigger than your silk and
to fit your ring frame
Stranded cottons:
Dark lime green
Medium lime green
Light lime green
Mustard
Nine gold seed beads
Pencil and tracing paper
Tacking thread
Pins
Needles: no. 9

Ring frame

*The pattern for the Climbing Leaves
project, shown full size.*

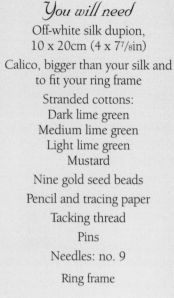

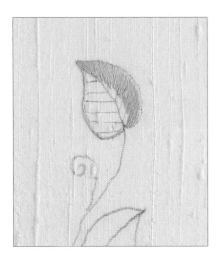  

1. Trace the design and mount the background fabric onto calico (see page 21). Using one strand of the light lime green thread, work in stem stitch around the top leaf. Draw on pencil lines to guide you. The angle of the stitches should be at about 45 degrees to the central stem. Work the lime green up one side of the leaf. Towards the tip of the leaf, fan the stitches out from one point. This is easier than trying to work tiny diagonal stitches and will give a much tidier effect. Remember to start in the middle of the leaf and stitch to the top, then return and work downwards.

2. Work the light green on the second side of the leaf. Fan the stitches out at the top to meet those from the other side. If necessary add a slightly longer stitch to define the tip of the leaf. Add in the medium lime green on to the first side. These should almost touch the central vein line in length. Work the second side of the leaf with the same colour.

3. Complete the first half with the dark lime green stitching down to the central vein. You can really exaggerate the long and short of the stitches here. As you are stitching in a smaller area, you will need fewer stitches, so take care where you place them.

4. Complete the second half of the leaf with the darkest lime green. Add a stem stitch down the middle of the leaf in two strands of mustard coloured thread. Continue this down the stem, adding in the little curls. Under each of the curls, stitch three gold seed beads. These are not on the tracing as it is difficult to cover a pencil mark with such a small bead, so refer to the finished design on page 26 for placing.

The finished Climbing Leaves project. See the Contents page for an autumnal version of the same design.

For this pincushion I worked the two leaves in different colours and added matching beads. I then brought the design together by stitching beads in both colours around the edge of the base.

You can rearrange the leaves and stems to create your own designs. I have created two different circular designs, one for the pincushion, also shown opposite, and one for this gold greetings card.

Tulip

Tulips are wonderful to embroider as they have big, open petals, and not too many of them! They come in a variety of colours, so you can choose your favourite. The colours within tulips are quite varied, and can be dramatic, for instance, red tulips often have a yellow base and black streaks. However, pink tulips tend to be more subtle with cream and white areas. This gives lots of scope for shading. The tulip I have worked in this project is an orangey, peachy colour and was growing in a window box in Bradford on Avon.

You will need

Very pale blue-grey silk dupion,
24 x 24cm (9½ x 9½in)

Calico, bigger than your dupion
and to fit your ring frame

Stranded cottons:
Very dark Coral
Dark coral
Mid coral
Light coral
Very light coral
Pale lemon
Mid lemon
Mid green
Light green

Pencil and tracing paper

Tacking thread

Pins

Needles no.9

Ring frame

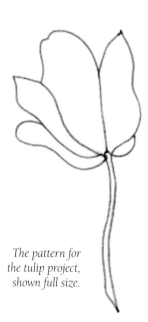

The pattern for the tulip project, shown full size.

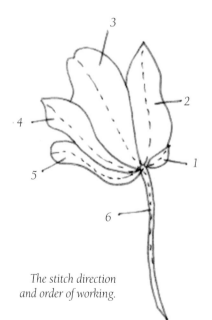

The stitch direction and order of working.

The areas of shading for the tulip.

1. All of this design is worked using 1 strand of thread. Start by stitching the tiny part of the petal showing on the far right (petal 1). Split stitch around it in mid coral. You only need to split stitch the outer edge where it is not touching any other petals. Work the bottom part of the petal, coming up in the fabric halfway up the area and going down where the petal joins the stem. You will need to work two rows in this shade. Add a few stitches of lemon in at the bottom. Finish the tip by coming up in the mid coral and down over the split stitch edge using very dark coral.

Split stitch around petal 2 in mid coral, starting at the bottom on the right-hand side, working all the way around to the point where it meets the edge of the next petal. Start shading at the bottom with the mid lemon, work one row, coming up in the fabric and down over the split stitch edge. Work a second row in pale lemon. This has a dip in the middle, so work slightly shorter stitches in the centre. This row is worked coming up in the mid lemon and down into the fabric. Shade mid coral into the yellow, echoing the dip in the middle. Work two rows using quite long stitches. Longer stitches always give a smoother overall effect. This will take you fairly near to the top of the petal, but as the other colours overlap, it is not a problem.

2. Finish petal 2 with one row of dark coral and one row of very dark coral. You may only have a very short row of the very dark coral, but do not worry about this, as its darkness will make it stand out.

Split stitch around petal 3 using pale coral.

Start at the bottom of the petal with pale lemon. Work this so that it is taller in the middle and lower at the sides, forming an arc shape with a small dip in the middle (see the pattern on the right on page 28). Shade a few stitches of mid lemon into the pale lemon to darken it slightly.

On the right edge, put in a few stitches of mid coral. This is so that the edge of this petal does not merge into the one next to it. On the left-hand edge of the petal work a slightly wider area of pale coral.

Shade into the pale lemon with very pale coral all the way across the petal. Work two rows in very pale coral. Continue up the left-hand side of the petal with the pale coral.

3. Shade the pale coral from the left-hand side across the petal, shading into the very pale coral. Try to echo the shape of the yellow shading. Then do the same with the mid coral. This may go over the split stitch edge at the top of the petal. Finish the top of the petal with a few dark coral stitches. Take these down the left-hand side making it fairly dark.

Split stitch around petal 4 in pale coral. Stitch all the way around to the point where it meets petal 5. Start at the bottom with mid lemon, then pale lemon. Work into this with pale coral, taking it down the left-hand edge. Work three rows, with it high on the right-hand side, covering the split stitch edge.

4. Work the final row up over the split stitch edge in mid coral. This is mainly off to the left-hand side and kept quite high up the petal.

Split stitch around petal 5 in pale coral. This time you can work all the way around the petal.

Start at the bottom with mid lemon, then shade into pale lemon. Watch the angle of the stitches here, as they start almost lying horizontal and need to work their way around the bend to more of a 45 degree angle. Shade into the pale lemon with mid coral. Work this to the top of the petal, leaving an area on the left for some dark coral. Add a few stitches of very dark coral into the left-hand edge.

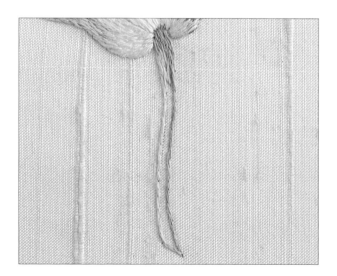

5. Split stitch all the way around the stem. Work the right-hand side in mid green, and the left-hand side in pale green.

Start shading at the top of the stem, coming up in the stem just below the top, and going down over the split stitch edge. The next row will come up in these stitches and work downwards, down the stem.

For the following rows add the pale green in on the left-hand side. Fleck the 2 colours in together in the middle where they meet and work all the way down the stem. Finish the stem off with mid green at the bottom.

The finished Tulip project, mounted with a double cream mount and framed. Card mounts add depth to your work and stop the glass from pressing against your stitching.

This is the same tulip design as the project, worked in bright reds and oranges.

Opposite

A different variety of tulip embroidered fairly small to fit the aperture of a notebook. This shows how tulip leaves can be worked.

Butterfly

Butterflies are great fun to stitch because of the colours on their wings, and there are no difficult angle changes.
They also give scope for inventing your own colour schemes. You can stitch imaginary butterflies, adding in glittery threads, beads and sequins, as I have on the embroidered bag on page 39. I spent an afternoon chasing butterflies in a local butterfly house, getting some great photographs of more exotic species. I printed these out in black and white so I could trace the basic shapes of the wings, bodies and different areas of colour, and then chose my own colours to stitch them in. The black and white pictures show where the shades change, so are really useful if you want to use different colours.

However the butterfly in this project is a real specimen shown in its true colours. I have just slightly simplified the body where the area is too small to stitch in too much detail.

You will need

Coffee/beige silk dupion, 20 x 20cm (7⁷/₈ x 7⁷/₈in)

Calico, bigger than your dupion and to fit your ring frame

Stranded cottons:

Dark mustard
Mustard
Dark brown
Tomato red
Dark orange
Orange
Cream
Chestnut brown

Pencil and tracing paper

Tacking thread

Pins

Needles: no.9

Ring frame

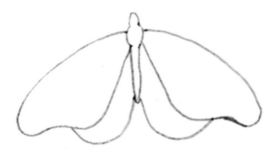

The outline for the butterfly project shown full size. As the antennae are stitched in a single stitch, it is best not to trace them on to the fabric, as covering the line with a single strand is very difficult.

These two patterns show the direction of stitching (left) and the areas of colour (right). They are three-quarters of actual size and are for guidance only.

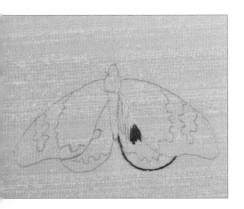

1. The bottom wings are underneath, so they are embroidered first. Split stitch around the wing from where it meets the body to where it meets the edge of the top wing using dark brown. Work an area of long and short stitch in dark mustard in the top corner of the wing. Work two rows. Angle the stitches almost straight downwards, but as the area gets wider, fan the stitches out slightly. You will need to add in extra stitches as the area gets bigger. Using dark brown, stitch a small area to the right. This will be a spot, so make sure the top edge of the stitching curves around. You do not need to worry about the bottom of the stitches, as they can be shaped when you come up into them with the row of stitches below.

2. Work underneath the dark brown spot with dark mustard. Shape it into a circular spot. Continue down the edge where the top wing meets the bottom wing with a row of dark mustard stitches. The stitches will need to get shorter as the area get smaller. Work into these stitches with a row of mustard stitches. On the edge nearest to the body they will begin to cover the split stitch edge.

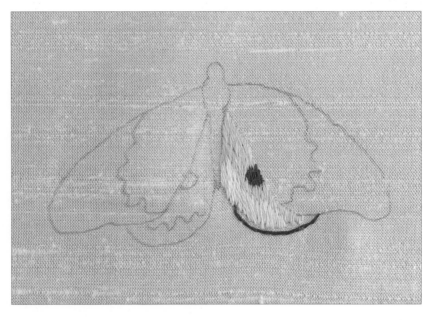

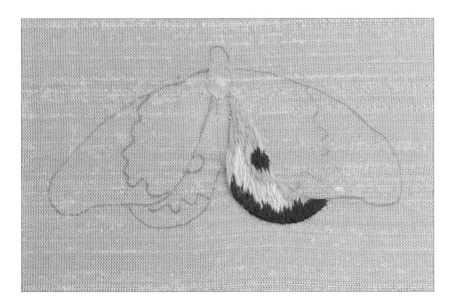

3. Finish the edge of the wing with dark brown. These stitches are small, but try to feather them into the mustard so that you do not get a solid line. Repeat on the other side of the butterfly, working the wings in exactly the same way, but as a mirror image. Do not worry too much if the two wings are not the same. I'm sure they are not identical in nature!

4. Split stitch all the way around the wing from where it leaves the body back to where it rejoins the body. Work a few rows of dark brown, two stitches wide, along the top line of split stitch. These are slightly angled so that they cover the split stitch edge. Next work a slim area of dark orange stitches going into the dark brown and down the wing. Work along the edge of this row with a larger block of tomato red stitches and then back into the dark orange.

5. Shade from the dark orange into orange to complete the top part of the wing. Shade across the bottom of this with dark orange, leaving a small gap on the left.

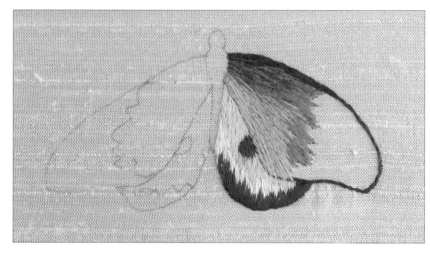

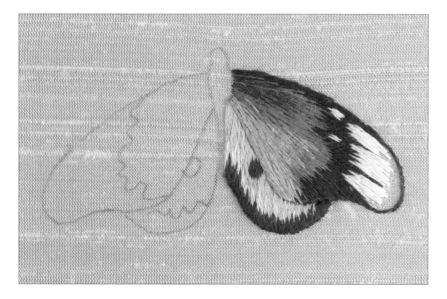

6. Starting back up on the top edge of the wing with dark brown, shade all the way along the edge of the oranges to the other side. Shape the top of these stitches so that two and half scallop shapes are formed in the orange. To the bottom left of the wing, work a second row of dark brown, taking it further down over the split stitch edge. Add in three areas of cream. These have a line of dark brown going down between them to separate them. Add a few cream flecks high up in the brown on the right-hand side of the wing.

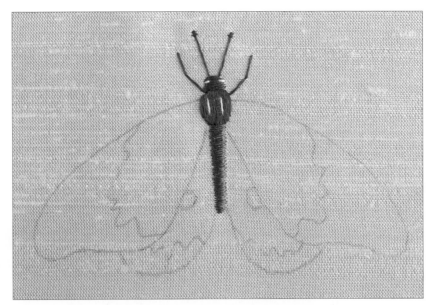

7. Finish the wing off in dark brown, shaping the ends of the cream areas into curves. Add in a few cream flecks at the tip of the wing and also further up on the left.

8. When all four wings are completed, split stitch around the top part of the body and the head in dark brown. (Note that the picture shows the wings unstitched for clarity.) As these are small, curved shapes you will need to use very small split stitches. Work up and over the split stitch, simply filling in the body with vertical stitches, then the head with horizontal stitches. You may find it easier to start in the middle and work in one direction first, then go back to the middle and work the other way. This will help you to keep the stitches at the angle you want them. In the centre of the middle section of the body, add two cream stitches to highlight it. Using the same thread, you can add in some tiny stitches either side of the head for eyes. Work the antennae and legs in single, long, dark brown stitches. Add a couple of tiny stitches at the end of the antennae. The long, thin part of the body is worked in chestnut brown. Split stitch around the shape and then work small horizontal stitches over it all the way down the shape.

The finished embroidery, shown larger than actual size for clarity.

The finished Butterfly project mounted in a dark, round frame to set off the vibrant colours.

Here a different variety of butterfly was worked on pale blue silk and stitched to the dark blue satin of a trinket box.

Opposite
This fun denim bag was embroidered with mystical, colourful butterflies embellished with small sequins, beads and metallic thread.

Dog Roses

This final project was inspired by the dog roses growing in a local hedgerow. I knew the flowers would be a great subject to embroider. Dog roses are ideal for shading as they have big, open petals and beautiful soft colours.

This project has been worked on a delicate green silk background to enhance the gentle colours in the shading. The whole design is worked in a single strand of thread.

You will need

Pale green silk dupion, at least
34 x 30cm (13½ x 11¾in)

Calico, bigger than your silk and
to fit your ring frame

Stranded cottons:
Dark pink
Medium pink
Light pink
White
Dark green
Medium green
Light green
Very light green
Soft yellow
Mustard

Pencil and tracing paper

Tacking thread and pins

Needles: no. 9

Ring frame

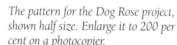

The pattern for the Dog Rose project, shown half size. Enlarge it to 200 per cent on a photocopier.

This pattern shows the order of stitching for the main flower and the stitch direction for the whole design. It is not full size and is for guidance only. The main rose on this design has five petals. You will see that this flower has two petals at the back, two in the middle and one at the front, with a turnover that is even further forward. Following the rule of working from the back forwards, the flower should be worked in that order. The leaves and stems of the design do not touch the rose or each other, so they can be worked in any order.

Main flower

1. Trace the design and mount the background fabric on to calico (see page 21). As this project is fairly large, it is best to tack the two fabrics together down and across the centre in addition to around the edges. This will stop the fabric from moving and should help avoid any puckering of the silk. Starting with the main rose, split stitch around the top edge of petal 1 in medium pink. Following the direction shown, start to shade the petal using the medium pink over the split stitch edge. Add in a few dark pink stitches along this edge and where it meets the petals on either side. Work on down the petal with light pink going into white at the flower centre. Remember to echo the outside shape of the petal with the shading. Finish the white neatly on the pencil line at the flower centre. Work petal 2 in the same way.

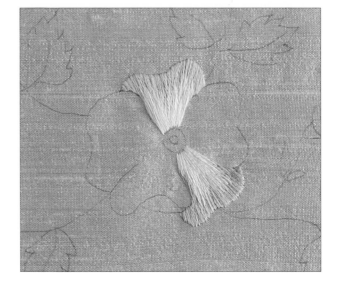

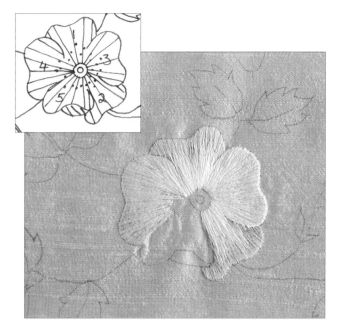

2. Petal 3 sits on top of petals 1 and 2, so it has a split stitch edge all the way around. Work the split stitch and start shading using pale pink. Add just a few flecks of medium pink, scattering them through the petal. Finish the petal in white, keeping the angle down the sides soft, so that although you are covering the split stitch edge, it is with an almost vertical stitch. This helps the petals blend together in the middle of the flower.

Petal 4 is worked with a split stitch edge from the point where it meets petal 5 around towards the base of petal 1 in light pink. Shade the right-hand side of the petal in light pink with flecks of medium pink, then into white. The left-hand side of the petal is a little darker with more medium pink down the edge where petal 5 overlaps.

3. Work a split stitch around petal 5 in light pink, but not the edge under the turnover. Shade the area just beneath the turnover with medium pink, working through light pink to a small amount of white towards the flower centre. Either side of the turnover, start shading in light pink and then white. Merge the areas together with a few medium pink stitches.

Split stitch all the way around the turnover in light pink. Working in small stitches, work the outer edge in medium pink, shading into light pink then finish the inside edge of the turnover (which is on top of the petal) in white.

Using the yellow, add in the filaments, varying their heights around the centre of the flower. Work the anthers on the ends of the filaments in French knots in mustard thread.

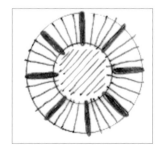
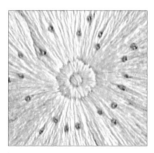

The diagram for the centre of the main flower.

4. For the centre, work split stitch in a circle around the bottom of the petals using yellow, and then a second one a few millimetres inside this. To get a nice curve you will need to work really tiny stitches. Stitch up and over the split stitch edges all the way around the circle centre, keeping the stitches at the correct angle (see diagram). You may find it helpful to put in a few guiding stitches first, to help you keep to the right angle. These are shown as darker lines on the diagram (left). Fill in the centre of the yellow circle with very light green stitches.

Leaves

There are four shades of green in this project. Some of the leaves
are worked in the darker three shades, and some in the lighter three
shades. Generally speaking, the leaves to the left of the stem are in the
darker three, and those to the right are in the lighter three.
All the leaves are worked with the darkest of their colours on the
outside edge, working into the paler shades in the middle. Split
stitching can always be worked in the darkest colour of that leaf.
Because of the shape of the leaves, it is easiest to work each little point
from its tip down one side, then take your needle back up to the tip
and work down the other side. Repeat this with the next tip, so that
the two then join up at the bottom. This is easier than trying to work
up and down the tips in one go.

Repeat with the next two shades, working in the same way, echoing
the outside shape of the leaf. The stitches should meet in the middle
on the central line.

5. Work the leaf on the left of the stem in dark green,
medium green and light green, as explained above.

6. Work the vein down the centre of the left-hand leaf
in medium green in stem stitch. Then work the right-
hand leaf in the same way, using medium green, light
green and very light green. All the stems joining the
flowers and leaves are worked in medium green and in
stem stitch.

Half open flower 1

7. Work the base of the flower, split stitching in medium green. Start shading with dark green, coming from under the base of the petals. Continue into medium green to complete the shape. Add a highlight of light green low down on the left-hand side. Work the small leaf to the left, split stitching the spiky edge with medium green and shading, starting with dark green coming out from under the petal into medium green over the edge.

The small leaf to the right is shaded using dark, medium and light green. The dark is down the centre and light around the edges.

Work the back two petals first, split stitching and working mainly in light pink. Work down into white. Add a few flecks of medium pink in with the light pink on the outer edge.

Add filaments into the white area using yellow and work the anthers in French knots using mustard thread.

Split stitch around the edges of the turnover and stitch the top area in medium pink. Shade into dark pink where it meets the front petal. Work the front, right-hand petal with the turnover first. The main part of the petal is worked in light pink with flecks of medium pink at the bottom and white under the turnover. Split stitch around in light pink. The turnover is worked in mainly dark pink, with a few medium flecks on the edge over the main petal.

Split stitch all the way round the final petal using medium pink. The top edge is worked in light pink. Shade into white and then back into light pink. The base of the petal near the leaf is worked in medium pink. Add in a few flecks of dark pink.

Half open flower 2

8. The leaves of the second half-open flower are split stitched around in light green. They are then worked in medium green coming out from under the flower and shaded into light green, with just a fleck of very light green on the tips.

Start with the small section of petal just peeking through at the back. Split stitch the small curve on the outside of the petal. Work in light pink and white, with just a few flecks of medium pink.

Work the central back petal, split stitching all the way around the outer edge in light pink and shade mainly in light pink and white, with flecks of medium pink.

The petals to the right and left are worked next, using medium pink more heavily, as well as light pink and white. The turnover of the right-hand petal is worked in dark and medium pink.

The final front petal is split stitched all the way around in dark pink and shaded with all the pinks and a small amount of white at the bottom.

Bud

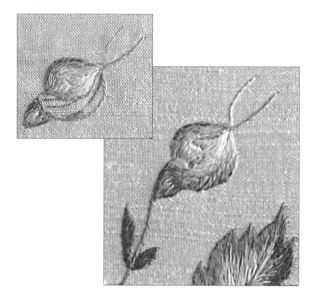

9. The pink of the bud is worked first with small amounts of light, medium and dark pink. Split stitch around the small green base of the bud in medium green and work with the three lighter shades of green. Start with the darkest coming from under the bud and down its sides. The smaller back sepal of the bud is also shaded using the three lighter shades of green with a slither of the medium green down the outside edge and the very light green where it sits over the pink. The fine tendril is worked in stem stitch in light green.

The front sepal is split stitched all the way around in light green and worked in the same way as the back one with a slither of medium on the outside edge and very light green next to the pink on the inside edge. The fine tendril is worked in stem stitch and in very light green. The small leaves on the main stem are worked in medium green.

Opposite

The finished Dog Rose project. Although this is a fairly large piece, I thoroughly enjoyed stitching it. If you do not fancy tackling such a large design, just work a small area of it. You could also use tracing paper to trace parts of it and rearrange them to form your own design.

Index